MACAWS AT RISK
SAVING THESE COLORFUL BIRDS

BY KATHRYN CLAY

CAPSTONE PRESS
a capstone imprint

Published by Capstone Press, an imprint of Capstone
1710 Roe Crest Drive, North Mankato, Minnesota 56003
capstonepub.com

Copyright © 2026 by Capstone. All rights reserved. No part of this publication may be reproduced in whole or in part, or stored in a retrieval system, or transmitted in any form or by any means, electronic, mechanical, photocopying, recording, or otherwise, without written permission of the publisher.

Library of Congress Cataloging-in-Publication Data is available on the Library of Congress website.

ISBN: 9798875221873 (hardcover)
ISBN: 9798875221828 (paperback)
ISBN: 9798875221835 (ebook PDF)

Summary: Macaws are clever and quick, but they are at risk of dying out. Readers will investigate the circumstances putting macaws at risk, including the illegal pet trade and habitat loss, as well as what people can do to help.

Editorial Credits
Editor: Ashley Kuehl; Designer: Elijah Blue; Media Researcher: Rebekah Hubstenberger; Production Specialist: Tori Abraham

Image Credits
Alamy: Graham Prentice, 28; Associated Press: Bénédicte Desrus/Sipa USA, 27; Getty Images: DjelicS, 24, iStock/Freder, 18, iStock/Jorge Roman Mendez Liska, 9, iStock/Ondrej Prosicky, 5, iStock/Sergio Garrido Garcia, 23, iStock/SeventyFour, 29, John Coletti, 22, Patrick Pleul/picture alliance, 21; Shutterstock: Alan Tunnicliffe, 14, CHUCHAT TREEPRAPHAKORN, 19, DeawSS, 4 (heart icon), Hugh Lansdown, 17, imranhridoy, 4 (trees icon), iulianbugasa, 13, Jiri Hrebicek, 16, Martin Mecnarowski, 12, Michael Fitzsimmons, 25, Miguel Schmitter, 7, nexusby, 4 (temperature icon), Ondrej Prosicky, cover, photomaster, 6, sarah_xie7, 15, Stefan Balaz, 4 (arrow icon), Tarcisio Schnaider, 11, Viktor Tanasiichuk, 11 (map), Vinicius Bacarin, 8

Design Elements
Pixels Park, Textures and backgrounds

Any additional websites and resources referenced in this book are not maintained, authorized, or sponsored by Capstone. All product and company names are trademarks™ or registered® trademarks of their respective holders.

TABLE OF CONTENTS

CHAPTER 1
A DAY IN THE LIFE 5

CHAPTER 2
GET TO KNOW MACAWS 10

CHAPTER 3
ENDANGERED 20

CHAPTER 4
HOW TO HELP 26

GLOSSARY 30
READ MORE 31
INTERNET SITES 31
INDEX 32
ABOUT THE AUTHOR 32

Words in **bold** are in the glossary.

WHAT MAKES AN ANIMAL ENDANGERED?

NUMBER OF ANIMALS:
VERY LOW OR SHRINKING FAST

HABITAT LOSS:
BIG DECREASE IN NATURAL HABITAT

RANGE REDUCTION:
SHRINKING AREA WHERE IT CAN LIVE

BREEDING DECLINE:
FEWER ANIMALS HAVING YOUNG

THREATS:
HIGH RISK OF POACHING, DISEASE, OR CLIMATE CHANGE

CHAPTER 1
A DAY IN THE LIFE

Colorful wings stand out against the leaves of the rainforest trees. With a loud call, a macaw takes flight. The bird soars swiftly through the trees in search of food. Using its sharp beak, the macaw cracks open tough nuts and seeds.

The macaw spends its day flying from tree to tree. By afternoon, it seeks out a safe spot high in the trees to rest and avoid danger. The macaw returns to its nest as evening approaches. In a hollow tree, the nest offers a safe place to sleep. Tomorrow the adventure will begin again.

Macaws are bright, colorful birds found in southern Mexico and Central and South America. They are the largest members of the parrot family. Macaws are known for their striking colors and long tails. Their loud calls are recognized throughout the rainforest.

Cockatiels, like macaws, are part of the parrot family.

MACAW TRIVIA

QUESTION: What other birds are parrots?

ANSWER: More than 350 species of parrots exist. Parakeets, lovebirds, and cockatiels are all parrots.

Red-and-green macaws fly through the Amazon Rainforest in Peru.

Macaws are social animals and often live in large **flocks**. These birds are active during the day. They call loudly to one another as they fly through the forest.

AT RISK

Macaws are facing **extinction** because of several threats. Habitat loss and climate change have reduced their natural homes. With fewer places to nest, macaws have fewer young.

Illegal hunters capture macaws for their feathers and meat. They also sell the birds as pets. **Conservation** efforts are underway to protect macaw habitats and prevent **poaching**. But without action, several **species** could soon face extinction.

A wild macaw in a cage after being caught by a poacher

Macaws rest on a city roof in Caracas, Venezuela.

CHAPTER 2
GET TO KNOW MACAWS

Wild macaws make their nests in tropical rainforests, near rivers, and along the coast. Some macaws also live in grassy areas or fields.

Macaws are often found high in the forest **canopy**. Their bright feathers blend in with the colorful rainforest plants. They build their nests more than 100 feet (30 meters) above the ground. This height provides easy access to food and safety from **predators**.

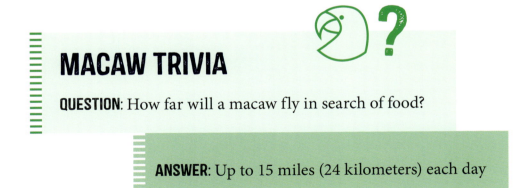

MACAW TRIVIA

QUESTION: How far will a macaw fly in search of food?

ANSWER: Up to 15 miles (24 kilometers) each day

BIRD BODIES

Macaws are known for their bright feathers. Many species are named for their feathers. These species include the blue-and-yellow macaw, scarlet macaw, and green-winged macaw.

Different species vary in size and weight. The smallest macaws weigh about 5 ounces (141 grams). The largest species is the hyacinth macaw. It weighs nearly 4 pounds (1.8 kilograms). Macaws range from 1 to 3.3 feet (0.3 to 1 m) long. Their tails can make up half of their body length.

A MACAW SHORT STORY

Write a story about a day in the life of a macaw.

1. **Gather Details**. Research what macaws eat, where they live, and how they interact with other birds.

2. **Choose a Setting**. Decide where your story takes place. Is it in the trees, near a river, or flying through the jungle?

3. **Create Your Character**. Give your macaw a name. Is it playful, scared, or curious? Describe its feathers and how it flies.

4. **Describe a Day.** What does your macaw do? Include details about its actions and environment.

5. **Add a Problem.** Introduce a challenge, such as a predator. How does your macaw respond?

6. **End the Story.** Your macaw might solve a problem, learn something new, or return home safely.

ONE POWERFUL BEAK

A macaw's beak is incredibly powerful. It can crack open tough nuts and seeds. Even coconut shells are no match for these birds. When threatened, macaws use their beaks to deliver sharp bites.

A beak also serves as a third foot. It helps the bird climb and grip branches. Beaks grow throughout their lives, just like human fingernails.

A military macaw uses its beak and foot to crack open a walnut.

BIRD FEET

Not all bird feet are the same. The most common type is called anisodactyl (an-ih-soh-DAK-tuhl). These feet have three toes pointing forward and one pointing backward. Robins, blue jays, and chickens have these feet.

Macaws have zygodactyl (zai-goh-DAK-tuhl) feet. They have two toes pointing forward and two pointing backward. These unique feet work like human hands. They help macaws grip objects, climb trees, and hold food while eating. Owls and woodpeckers also have zygodactyl feet.

BONDED FOR LIFE

Macaws are highly social birds. They often travel in pairs or flocks of up to 30 other birds. Their loud squawks and screeches can be heard over long distances. The sounds are used to talk and warn of danger.

Macaws form strong, lifelong bonds with their mates. Bonded pairs are rarely apart. Even in a flock, they fly side by side with wings nearly touching. Bonded macaws share food and groom each other. They even lick each other's faces and hold hands (feet).

A pair of bonded macaws fly through a Brazilian rainforest.

MACAW TRIVIA

QUESTION: How wide is a macaw's wingspan (its outstretched wings)?

ANSWER: A hyacinth macaw's wingspan can reach 4 to 5 feet (1.2 to 1.5 m).

LIFE CYCLE

The life cycle of macaws begins with an egg. Nests are built inside trees. A female lays one to four eggs. She sits on them for about a month. The male brings her food. Chicks are born blind and featherless. They rely on their parents for warmth and food.

A newborn scarlet macaw hatched in captivity.

Macaw chicks resting in their nest

In 10 weeks to three months, the young birds become more independent. They grow feathers and begin to fly. They'll stay with their parents for at least a year.

MACAW TRIVIA

QUESTION: What is a macaw's lifespan?

ANSWER: Macaws can live up to 60 years in the wild. They can live even longer in captivity.

CHAPTER 3
ENDANGERED

Animals are at risk when not many of them are left. Without protection, **endangered** animals may become extinct. This means they disappear completely. Once something goes extinct, it can't be brought back.

Many macaw species are endangered. Others are close to extinction. For nearly 20 years, the Spix's macaw was only found in captivity. Scientists were able to breed them. In 2022 they released 20 of these birds back into the wild.

CONSERVATION ON THE BIG SCREEN

The movie *Rio* (2011) is about protecting macaws. The main bird, Blu, is a Spix's macaw. He's nearly the last of his kind. Blu is captured by poachers. He goes on an adventure to help protect other macaws. The movie is fun, but it also raises awareness about risks to macaws.

A pair of Spix's macaws in a German conservation center in 2018

ENVIRONMENTAL RISKS

Environmental factors pose the greatest threat to macaws. Rainforests are being cut down. Trees once home to macaws are used for construction materials. Pineapple and palm oil plantations take their place. This **deforestation** destroys nesting sites and food sources.

A pineapple plantation in Costa Rica.

Losing trees means macaws lose their homes inside those trees.

Climate change can cause warmer temperatures or changes in rainfall. Weather changes cause droughts, flooding, and fires. These changes harm the plants and trees that macaws need for food and shelter. Losing trees makes it harder for these birds to survive.

HUMAN-MADE RISKS

Humans also harm macaws. People take the birds from the wild to sell them. Macaws' bright colors and sounds make them popular pets. Each bird can sell for thousands of dollars. The high price encourages even more poaching.

A veterinarian with an *Ara ararauna*, or blue-and-yellow, macaw

Sometimes macaws are captured for their feathers and meat. The feathers are used in special ceremonies or clothing. Some people are trying to help. They collect feathers from zoos and people who breed macaws legally. They give away these feathers, in hopes that it stops people from hunting wild birds.

Macaw feathers are rare and valuable.

PET LAWS

In the United States, more than 40 million parrots are kept as pets. U.S. laws require macaws to be hatched and raised in the United States. Such laws prevent the illegal capture and sale of wild macaws.

CHAPTER 4
HOW TO HELP

There are several ways to help protect macaws. First, it's important to protect their habitats. Stopping deforestation in rainforests is key. Some programs buy land to protect it from being cut down. People plant new trees in areas that have been destroyed. They want to make sure macaws have a safe and healthy habitat. Supporting conservation programs can make a big difference.

MACAW TRIVIA

QUESTION: How fast can a macaw fly?

ANSWER: Macaws can reach speeds of 35 miles (56 km) per hour.

Mayan women in Mexico replant mangrove trees in areas where they have been cut down.

GROUPS WORKING TO HELP MACAWS

Macaw Recovery Network manages breeding programs meant to restore wild macaw populations.

Parrots International funds research, breeding programs, and habitat-protection projects worldwide.

World Parrot Trust works with local partners to educate communities and stop illegal trading.

Local communities can protect macaws with **ecotourism**. Tourists pay to see the birds in their natural environments. Money from tourism creates jobs. Locals can also use tourist money to buy land to create protected animal habitats.

Stopping illegal wildlife trade would be a huge help to macaws. People can learn about anti-poaching laws. They can raise awareness about the effects of buying macaws as pets. Teaching people about these dangers inspires people around the world to help save macaws.

The Buraco das Araras is a famous macaw habitat near Jardim, Brazil.

Awareness Poster

Make a poster to help raise awareness about macaws.

1. **Research Macaws.** Find out what people are doing to help protect them and their habitats.

2. **Create a Slogan.** Come up with a catchy phrase that invites people to help raise awareness about macaws. One example is: "Explore the Wild, Save the Macaws!"

3. **Design a Poster.** Draw pictures of macaws and the rainforest. Describe how people are helping macaws. Include your slogan.

4. **Share.** Present your poster to family, friends, and classmates.

GLOSSARY

canopy (KAN-uh-pee)—the upper layer of a rainforest where the greenery is thick

conservation (khan-sur-VAY-shun)—wise use and protection of natural resources

deforestation (dee-for-uh-STAY-shun)—cutting down or clearing large areas of trees and forests

ecotourism (ee-koh-TOOR-is-uhm)—visiting a place that has unspoiled natural resources, while being careful to have minimal impact on the environment

endangered (en-DANE-jurd)—at risk of dying out

extinction (ik-STINGKT-shuhn)—when no members of a species are still living; an extinct animal has died out

flock (FLAHK)—a group of the same kind of animal; members of flocks live, travel, and eat together

poaching (POHCH-ing)—illegal hunting or fishing

predator (PRED-uh-tur)—an animal that hunts other animals for food

species (SPEE-sheez)—a group of plants or animals that share common characteristics

READ MORE

Bodden, Valerie. *Parrots.* Mankato, MN: The Creative Company, 2023.

McMurdie, Becca. *Building a Beak: How a Toucan's Rescue Inspired the World.* Salem, MA: Page Street Kids, 2024.

Perdew, Laura. *Your Sustainable World: A Kid's Guide to Everyday Choices that Help the Planet!* North Mankato, MN: Capstone Press, 2025.

INTERNET SITES

Macaw
animals.sandiegozoo.org/animals/macaw

Threatened Species
macawrecoverynetwork.org/the-network/threatened-species/

Weird But True: Birds
kids.nationalgeographic.com/weird-but-true/article/birds

INDEX

beaks, 5, 14

calls, 5, 6, 7, 16, 24
chicks, 4, 8, 18, 19
climate change, 4, 8, 23
conservation, 8, 20, 21, 25, 26, 27, 28, 29

deforestation, 22, 23, 26

ecotourism, 28

feathers, 8, 10, 12, 13, 19, 25
feet, 14, 15, 16
flocks, 7, 16
food, 5, 10, 11, 13, 14, 15, 16, 18, 22, 23

habitats, 4, 8, 26, 27, 28, 29

life cycle, 18, 19

mates, 16

nests, 5, 8, 10, 18, 19, 22

pets, 8, 24, 25, 28
poaching, 4, 8, 20, 24, 25, 28
predators, 10, 13

rainforests, 5, 6, 7, 10, 16, 22, 26, 29
Rio, 20

size, 12

ABOUT THE AUTHOR

Kathryn Clay has written more than 100 nonfiction books for kids. Her books cover a wide range of topics, including everything from sign language to space travel. When she's not writing, Kathryn works at a college, helping students develop their critical thinking and study skills. She holds master's degrees in literature and creative writing from Minnesota State University, Mankato.

Kathryn lives in southern Minnesota with her family and an energetic goldendoodle. Together, they make sustainable, eco-friendly choices whenever possible.